KIDDING AROUND

Los Angeles

A YOUNG PERSON'S GUIDE TO THE CITY

JULY CASH

ILLUSTRATED BY JIM FINNELL

John Muir Publications

Santa Fe, New Mexico

1. What Is this Place Called Los Angeles?

Los Angeles is a high-spirited, casual city with year-round nice weather and a relaxed life-style combined with a touch of Hollywood Glitz and a reputation as a playground for adults. For kids, it provides an almost endless supply of fun.

In L.A. you can ride the boards (skate, surf, boogie, or skim), rent a bike or a horse, take a cruise or a helicopter ride.

In L.A. you can discover an entire universe in a small pool of water at low tide, watch pelicans dive for their supper, and maybe see a whale on his way to Mexico or Alaska.

In L.A. you can see historic buildings, futuristic buildings, and buildings that look like ocean liners or hot dogs. And you can visit museums where you are encouraged to touch, where you can play with a robot, work in a TV station, or pretend to be an astronaut.

In L.A. you can pass celebrities on the street, watch a movie being made, and be in the studio audience of your favorite TV show.

In L.A. you can visit an enormous cactus garden that makes you feel like you're on another planet, smell a thousand rose bushes in full bloom, and sit under a tree covered with a million butterflies.

There are 1,500 miles of freeways and 12,500 miles of surface streets in Los Angeles County. There are 5,223,100 registered vehicles.

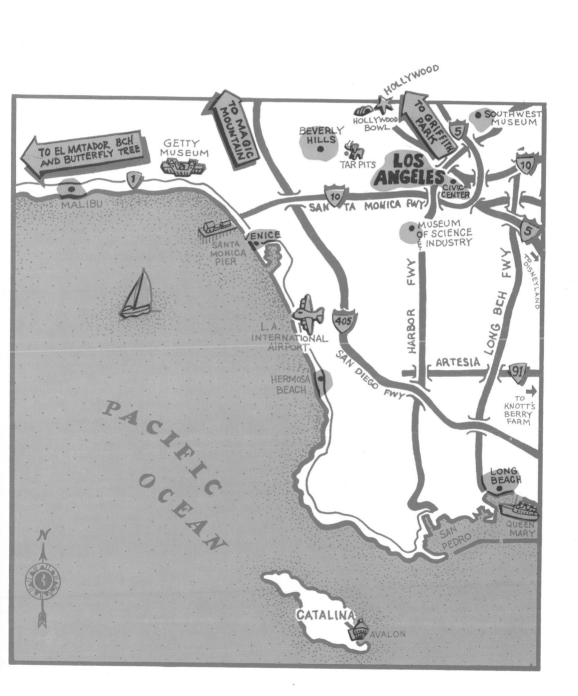

Cars and trucks are not the only reasons for the smog in Los Angeles. Oil refineries, power plants, and other industries also contribute to the brown air. The problem is balancing the need for the energy and power that makes everything work against the need for clean, healthy air. Many cities are trying to cope with this dilemma. Is it a problem in your hometown? Do you know how people there are trying to solve it?

In L.A. you can watch McEnroe play Lendl and see a Laker game, a Dodger game, a horse race, a boxing match, or a rodeo. Or how about a rock concert, a ballet, or a puppet show?

L.A. is the second biggest city in the United States. It has a beach at its front door, mountains in its backyard, and sunshine most of the time. And it is very spread out; in fact, Los Angeles County covers 4,083 square miles.

Which brings up one of the problems with L.A.: there is not a good system for public transportation. So the roads and freeways are crowded with cars, all spewing 7,200 tons of pollutants into the air every day and creating L.A.'s famous smog. It is a fact of life and one that Angelenos are very concerned about. There is a subway system being built, but it won't be in operation for several years.

A good map is absolutely essential for finding your way around. The best one, the one that people who live here use is the **Thomas Guide,** really a book of maps with a different section of L.A. on each page. You can buy one at any newsstand, bookstore, or hotel gift shop.

It is important to plan your sightseeing before you get in the car. Find out where things are, and visit places that are near each other on the same day. (Phone numbers are included for every place mentioned, so you can call ahead and ask for directions.) Remember, it will take longer than you think to get there, so leave early and find things to do in the car.

You will find that people in Los Angeles are usually very friendly and helpful to visitors, maybe because almost everyone came from somewhere else originally. Many people have come from very far away, leaving their own countries because of war, political persecution, or lack of jobs. They bring their own cultures, languages, traditions, and food and help to make L.A. a very exciting city. Have you ever stopped to think about what it would be like to leave your country and start all over again in a new place with a different language and strange customs?

Your visit to Los Angeles can be a wonderful adventure that you can start planning right now. This book gives you a preview of the possibilities so you can decide what interests you the most. Have a great trip!

The first gas station in the United States opened in L.A. in 1912.

Almost 8 million people live in Los Angeles.

There are 20,000 lawyers, 86,000 real estate salespeople, 62,000 actors, and a quarter of a million surfers.

2. A Brief History

When Spanish explorers "discovered" the area in 1769, Indians had been living here for centuries. In fact, they "discovered" a group of Shoshoni Indians living by a river in a village called Yang-na on the site of what is now downtown Los Angeles. The Spanish named the place Pueblo del Rio de Nuestra Señora la Reina de los Angeles, or River Town of Our Lady, the Queen of the Angels. That mouthful was soon shortened to Los Angeles and these days is often shortened even more to just L.A.

At the time of the discovery, Mexico was ruled by Spain, and the Spanish government soon sent people up from Mexico to colonize the area. Those who came were mostly people who didn't have much going for them in Mexico and who were looking for a better life. Priests and other religious people also came and set up missions. The missions had all the power of the Spanish government behind them. Their purpose was to give support to the settlers and, most important, to convert the Indians to Christianity and to European ways of doing things.

The newcomers, who became known as Californios, began to thrive in the warm climate

Los Angeles has almost no water supply of its own. Most of the water comes through a pipeline and travels more than 600 miles from central California. Some water comes from as far away as the Colorado River.

with the rich soil. More and more people came, including some Americans who were beginning to explore the west. Then Mexico fought the Spanish, gained its independence, and claimed the California territory as part of Mexico. The United States wanted California for its own and fought a war with Mexico to get it. By 1848, California was part of the United States.

It was right about then that gold was discovered near San Francisco and the Gold Rush was on. People from the east began pouring into California. Twenty years later, the cross-country railroad was completed, making the long journey to the west a little easier and, as competition between railroad companies grew, quite inexpensive. In 1885, you could take the train from Mississippi to Los Angeles for only one dollar.

Thousands of people came looking for a better life and many became farmers, planting thousands of acres of orange trees and other crops. Then just before the turn of the century, Los

There are streets and places with Spanish names all over Los Angeles.

La Tijera Blvd. = Scissors Blvd.

La Brea Ave. = Tar Ave.

Hermosa Beach = Beautiful Beach

Redondo Beach = Round Beach

Playa del Rey = King's Beach

La Cienega Blvd. = Swamp Blvd.

Ventura Freeway = Good Fortune Freeway

Los Feliz Blvd. = The Happy Blvd.

Alameda Ave. = Shady Park Ave.

Palos Verdes = Green Sticks

Angeles discovered its own gold mines in the form of "black gold," or oil. Money poured out of the wells, more people came to take part in the action, and Los Angeles began to spread out.

At about the same time, the folks from the east who were involved in the new art of making movies discovered that the climate and the scenery were perfect for them. Before long Hollywood was on its way to becoming the movie capital of the world. In the beginning, many of the locals were not thrilled with the crazy artists from the east and it was not uncommon to see signs that said "No Dogs, No Actors." But the movie business flourished, especially during the Depression when Americans wanted something to take their minds off their troubles, and soon the newcomers were just another part of the melting pot that Los Angeles was becoming.

During World War II, Los Angeles became a center for manufacturing aircraft and today remains home to many aerospace companies. It is also a center of business, banking, and world trade, especially trade with the Far East.

Maybe because so many people have come here to start their lives over again, there is a spirit of adventure among Angelenos and a feeling that it's okay to do things a little differently, to explore new ways of thinking and living. That's why some folks think of it as a kind of a crazy place. Maybe it is. It is certainly a little different, and that's why it can be so much fun.

3. Hooray for Hollywood

When you say "Los Angeles," most people immediately think **Hollywood**—movie stars, glamour, and show business. In the old days the entertainment business was centered in the area known as Hollywood. Today the studios and networks are spread all over town. But it is still fun to visit the famous **Mann's Chinese Theater** on Hollywood Boulevard where the footprints and handprints of famous movie stars are imbedded in the concrete. When you walk along Hollywood Boulevard, look down—you are on the **Walk of Fame,** where the names of over 1,800 celebrities from films, TV, and music are engraved in bronze stars set in the sidewalk. And if you look up in the hills behind Hollywood Boulevard, you will see the famous **Hollywood Sign**.

There are many companies offering tours of well-known sights and movie stars' houses. If you are a real fan of old stars and legends, a tour might be interesting. But it's not really necessary because you can visit most of the places on your own. While you are in the area, someone might come up to you and ask if you would like to go to the taping of a TV show, usually a game show. They take you to the studio in a van and bring you back when it's over. You might want to go if

The famous HOLLYWOOD sign was originally an advertisement for a housing development called Hollywoodland. It was lit at night by 4,000 light bulbs. A custodian lived in a little cabin hidden behind the first L.

It costs $3,500 to put a
star on Hollywood
Boulevard—and the star
has to pay for it!

The hot fudge sundae was
invented at C.C. Brown's
Ice Cream Shop, still at
7007 Hollywood
Boulevard.

Three movie stars who
don't have a star on Hollywood Boulevard: Cher,
Jack Nicholson, and Jane
Fonda.

you like the show and have the time right then,
but there are many other ways to see TV shows
or movies being made.

If you want to watch a movie being made, then
Hollywood On Location is for you. On location
means that it is being shot somewhere around
town, not in a studio. Every day at 9:30 a.m.,
Hollywood On Location publishes a complete
list of all the movie and TV shows (even music
videos) that are being filmed around town that
day. It mentions what stars are involved and
gives the exact address, the times, whether it is
inside or out, and what special effects or stunts
are planned. It usually lists about 35 different
locations within 10 miles of Hollywood. You pay
$29 for a package containing all this information
plus detailed maps and directions. You can spend
an hour or a whole day on location, and it is the
best way to see what is really involved in making
a film. One thing you will learn is that it is a
slow process. It takes time to set up cameras,
lights, microphones, and actors between "takes"
(when the actual filming is done). So be prepared
to stand around and wait a lot, but there will be
plenty to see while you're waiting. You can
reserve your package by calling 213-659-9165,
but you have to go to the On Location office at
8644 Wilshire Boulevard in Beverly Hills to pick
it up. The office is fun—lots of pictures of happy
customers with the stars, Hollywood souvenirs,
and even an old-fashioned soda fountain.

You can also be in the audience of your favorite network TV show when it is taped in the studio. Call the particular network and ask for
information and reservations. Tapings are always
free. Telephone numbers: **ABC** 818-506-0067;
CBS 213-852-4002; **NBC** 818-840-3537; and
FOX 213-856-1000.

13

Looking like a stack of records on a record player, the first circular office building in the United States was the Capitol Records building, still on Vine Street near Hollywood Boulevard. After it was completed, it was discovered that one small detail had been forgotten: there was not one single closet in the entire building.

NBC also offers a **Studio Tour** of its facilities at 3000 West Alameda Avenue in Burbank. The tour includes the basement where all the sets (including the Wheel of Fortune), props, and costumes are stored, the set of the local news show, and a visit to the studio where the Tonight Show is filmed. You also go into a mini-studio where you can see yourself on camera and watch a demonstration of how special effects are made. You'll find out about the blue background that lets you fly like Superman. Tickets for the tour are $6.50 for adults, $4.50 for children under 12. Children 5 and under get in free. Call 818-840-3537 for more information.

You can spend a whole day in a real movie studio with the **Universal City Studios Tour** located not far from Burbank in Universal City. This is a working studio where you will see actors and actresses (maybe even a star) dressed in costume, going to work. The guided part of the tour lasts about 2 hours and takes you on an open tram through the "back lot"—a fantasy place with streets that look exactly like New York or Paris or an old western town. During the trip, all kinds of extraordinary things happen: you are attacked by Jaws and King Kong and miraculously survive a flash flood and an avalanche. In the meantime, you are learning about "special effects," the way movies make things look real when they are not real at all. You will see how they do stunts, too; people jumping from burning buildings, high speed car chases, and other movie illusions. The entrance to Universal Studios is at the junction of the Hollywood Freeway and Lankershim Boulevard. The phone number for information and directions is 818-508-9600. Tickets cost $18.95 for everyone over 12, $12.95 for kids 3-11. Chil-

dren under 3, free. Open every day except
Thanksgiving and Christmas.

A completely different view of a movie studio
is offered by **Burbank Studios** near NBC in Burbank. No big show here, just a working studio
where you can see how movies and TV shows are
really put together and watch the people who
really make it all happen making it happen.
What you see depends on what is going on the
day you are there, but you usually get to visit a
set where filming is actually happening. The
tours are small, no more than 12 people, and cost
$22 per person. There are two catches: children
under 10 are not permitted, and you have to
make a reservation at least a week in advance.
Write The Burbank Studios, 4000 Warner Boulevard, Burbank, CA 91522, or call 818-954-1744.

*Universal Studios is the
biggest movie studio in
the world, with more
than 500 buildings on 420
acres. There are even 50
acres of parking spaces.*

*The house from the TV
show Happy Days is at
565 N. Cahuenga Avenue
in Hollywood.*

The most expensive rental car in the world is a Lambourghini Countash for $750 a day from Beverly Hills Budget-Rent-A-Car.

If you want to get a feeling for the glamorous life of the very rich, check out **Beverly Hills**. You can visit the very expensive shops on **Rodeo Drive** (pronounced ro-*day*-o around here) and the surrounding streets. You will find gorgeous things, ugly·things, and silly things, all very expensive. You might very well see a celebrity or two, and you will certainly see a lot of other tourists looking for celebrities. You can also buy a map that tells you the addresses of famous people and you can drive by their houses. You'll probably just see a lot of big lawns and locked gates, but if you are a real stargazer, you'll enjoy it. The thing to remember is that in L.A. you might see your favorite star anywhere—walking down the street, at the movies, the beach, or a concert, even at the grocery store.

4. The Coast

T

Los Angeles has 74 miles of beach, supervised by more than 500 lifeguards.

Always swim near a lifeguard. You know a lifeguard is on duty when the flag is flying and the windows in his little house are open.

he beach is one of the best things about Los Angeles. Even if you don't like swimming or it isn't warm enough to go in the water, the beach is still the place for fun. Like L.A. itself, the beach is big and spread out. Different things happen at different beaches along the coast, so let's go through them all, starting at the north and working our way south.

The northern tip of the bay is **Point Dume**, really a tall sand and rock hill sticking out into the bay which you can see for miles as you drive up the coast. This can be a magic place. As you climb up the hill you will notice exactly how it is made—a core of solid rock is covered by a thick layer of sand that is held on by the plants and grasses that grow out of it. Where the plants are worn away, the sand disappears and you can see the rock core. (Be sure to stay on the trail so you don't kill any plants.) Below you there will probably be dolphins and ducks playing in the water and lots of seagulls and pelicans.

And Point Dume is a great place for **whale watching**. In the fall the whales leave their home territory in Alaska before the water freezes over and swim all the way down to Mexico to spend

Lifeguards communicate with surfers by flags. A yellow flag with a black dot, the "meatball flag," flying above the lifeguard stand means no surfing allowed. Checkered flags planted apart in the sand means surf only between the signs.

the winter in the warm bays. In the spring they head back up the coast to their Alaskan homes. Going in both directions, many whales pass right by Point Dume. You can often see them "spouting" a huge spray of water into the air or "breaching" (rising completely out of the water, tail up, twisting to the side and falling back). Sometimes they even poke their heads out of the water to look around. It is very exciting to watch these enormous animals doing their thing in the wild.

Whale-watching time is December through March, and you can go to Point Dume any time during the day. On weekends in February and March, park rangers are available to give information and to answer your questions. To find out exact dates and times, call 818-888-3770. It is an easy climb up the hill, although it is not accessible to wheelchairs or strollers. Another way to see whales is to take a boat on a whale-watching cruise. (Read more about that in chap. 5.) To get

to Point Dume, take Pacific Coast Highway up the Malibu coast. Half a mile past the signal light at Heathercliff Road, turn left on to Westward Beach Road and follow it all the way to the end.

Just to the north of Point Dume is a huge public beach called **Zuma Beach**, a great place for swimming or sunning. But less than 4 miles up the road to the north, there is another magic place, **El Matador State Beach**. Most people who live in Los Angeles don't even know about this place, and the entrance is small so keep your eyes out and follow the sign. You park on the hill and walk down the walkway (again, no wheelchairs or strollers) to the beach below. There are huge boulders you might want to try climbing. If you walk to the right (north), past the cave, you will discover an excellent place to go **tidepooling**. If you look closely, you will see that they are full of little sea creatures. There are anemones waving their many blue arms in the waves, crabs, starfish, sea urchins (be careful of their sharp spikes), tiny fishes, and sea hares, dark brown snaillike creatures without shells.

The more you look into the pools, the more you will see. Wear old tennies for walking on the rocks. Remember: everything is alive, so be respectful and don't take anything out of the pools. It's OK to turn over rocks to see the creatures underneath, but be sure to replace them.

You can only see the tidepools at low tide. There are usually two low tides in 24 hours, but the times change every day. You can find out when low tide is by looking on the weather page of the newspaper or by calling the Los Angeles County Lifeguard Station at 213-451-8761.

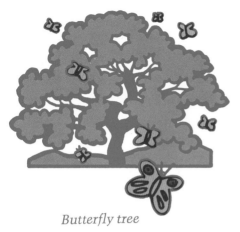

Butterfly tree

Would you like to go to a **grunion run**? *Then head for the beach at high tide on certain nights from March to July. That's when thousands of female grunion wiggle and jump and squirm their way onto the beach to lay their eggs in the wet sand. Each one buries herself in the sand to lay up to 3,000 eggs. Then she covers them with sand and throws herself back to the water. It's amazing to see this huge mass of little fish shimmering in the moonlight. To find out when the next run will be, call the lifeguards at 213-451-8761. Bring a flashlight.*

If you happen to be in L.A. between November and February and drive about 10 miles north of El Matador, you can see a kind of a miracle, and a secret one at that. It's the **butterfly tree** at **Sycamore Canyon.** Every year several million butterflies fly all the way from Canada to spend the winter at this particular tree. At first you don't notice, but after a minute you realize that every inch of the tree is covered and that the sky above is clouded with orange and black Monarch butterflies. Just sit under the tree and enjoy a once-in-a-lifetime sight. To find the secret tree, take Pacific Coast Highway north from El Matador to Sycamore Canyon. Turn right and follow the signs to the Campground. Turn left at the guard gate and then right into the parking lot. At the end of the parking lot there is a trail. The sign says HIKE/BIKE/CAMPING. Follow the trail for less than 50 yards to a barbecue area. Be still and look up.

Driving south down the coast along Pacific Coast Highway, you will soon be in the heart of **Malibu**, famous as a playground for movie stars and other celebrities. In fact, many of the houses on the cliffs above the tidepools and along the road belong to famous people. Most of the coast in Malibu is jammed with houses, one next to the other, but there are some public beaches. You can be among millions of birds at **Malibu Lagoon** or among what seems like millions of surfers at **Surfrider State Beach**. You can watch from the beach or walk out on the **Malibu Pier** for a different view. From sunrise to sunset, winter or summer, there are almost always people surfing. If you're there at low tide, you'll find some nice tidepools.

There are tidepools and surfers, too, at Topanga Beach. At low tide, this is also a good place to walk up the beach and see the ocean side of the houses along the highway. At high tide, there is no place to walk because the houses are almost in the water. That is because of erosion, which means that the sand has been washing away little by little. One reason for this is that instead of plants to hold the sand, there are wall-to-wall houses. Another reason is that coastlines are always changing, one beach gets smaller and another gets larger. That's the way it works. Sometimes people forget about that.

South of Malibu along the coast is **Santa Monica**, a great place to spend the day at the beach. There are lots of lifeguards and volleyball courts and playground equipment. There is a sidewalk

Malibu is a Chumash Indian word that means "where the mountain meets the sea," a perfect description of the Malibu coast.

Most of the outside scenes in the television show M*A*S*H were filmed at Malibu Canyon State Park.

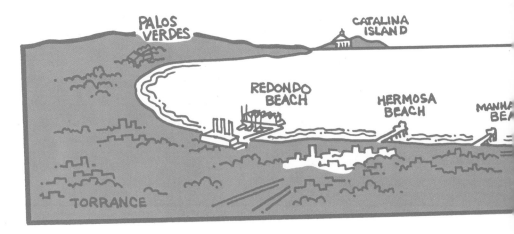

It is not a good idea to go to Malibu on a summer weekend or holiday because the traffic can be overwhelming. There is only one road, Pacific Coast Highway, so there is no way to get out of the traffic jam. The drive can take hours.

running along the beach where you can ride a bike or roller skate. One of the best things to do here is to go to **Santa Monica Pier** at the end of Colorado Avenue, the only pier that has rides and games, shops and restaurants. Be sure to take a ride on the famous **Carousel**, one of the nicest you will ever see with beautiful handpainted horses.

A couple of miles farther south is **Venice**, a most unusual place. In the summer and on sunny weekends and holidays, Venice is a funny, crazy scene. People go to Venice to watch other people. There are street musicians, clowns, and comedians, dancing roller skaters, and weight lifters. Sometimes there is a man who juggles chainsaws—while they are running! Vendors sell everything from earrings to socks and sunglasses of every imaginable design. Have your fortune told or your aura balanced, eat to your heart's content, and do it all right next to the beach. There is no place quite like Venice.

If you are interested in boats, you might want

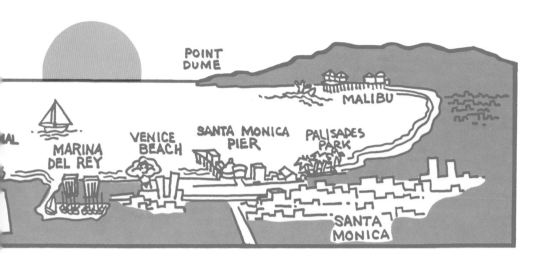

to go a little farther south to **Marina del Rey**. One of the largest marinas on the West Coast, it has more than 10,000 boats. You can walk around near the docks, or you can take a 40-minute cruise around the marina on an excursion boat called the Marina Belle. The boat leaves every hour on the hour from 11:00 a.m. until 4:00 p.m. seven days a week. It costs $6 for adults, $5 for kids 6-12, and $4 for those younger than 6. Call 213-822-1151 for reservations or information.

The area on the other side of the airport is known as the South Bay, and there are three little towns right next to each other, **Manhattan Beach, Hermosa Beach,** and **Redondo Beach.** The sidewalk, known in this area as "the Strand," runs for miles along the beach. Except for summer weekends, it's usually not very crowded. There are several places near the Strand to rent bikes, skates, and boogie boards (short little surfboards for riding the waves on your tummy). In the summer, there are professional volleyball tournaments with the best players from all over the country competing for thousands of dollars in prize money. They are free and open to the public.

Venice was developed at the beginning of this century by a man named Albert Kinney who wanted to create a city of canals, like Venice, Italy. He carved the canals and people came and built houses and fancy hotels. Venice was a very popular resort until oil was discovered under the sand. Soon the houses gave way to oil derricks and spills polluted the beach. Today there are a few canals left, with a year-round population of ducks, in a residential area very close to the beach. To see them, walk 3 blocks away from the beach on Washington St. or Venice Blvd.

23

5. San Pedro and Long Beach

T he San Pedro-Long Beach Area has so much to do and see that you can easily spend a day there. Your first stop should be the **Cabrillo Marine Museum** at 3720 Stephen White Drive. This is a small, very friendly place where you will get a close-up view of many fascinating sea creatures, including a whole tank full of baby sharks. You will learn how the ocean and the tides work and touch the inhabitants of the tidepool tank. This is the place to find out about the animals you have seen in the tidepools. (If you haven't had a chance to visit tidepools yet, now is the time because there is a big tidepool area at the beach right next to the museum.) Sometimes on weekends the museum people give guided tours of the tidepools which are a lot of fun. Call before you go to find out about that and other special events for kids (213-548-7562).

After the museum you will want to visit the nearby **Ports of Call Village**, at the foot of 6th Street, at San Pedro Harbor. If you're interested in ships and maritime history, stop in at the **Los Angeles Maritime Museum**, at the entrance to the village, where there are models and exhibits and lots af sailing memorabilia.

A breakwater is a barrier built in the water to protect the shore from waves. The breakwater that protects the harbors at San Pedro and Long Beach is 9 miles long and took 16 years to build.

By then you will probably be hungry. There are many restaurants to choose from in the Ports of Call Village. You can eat out on the deck, which has a great view of the comings and goings in the harbor. There are all kinds of shops to explore, but the most fun thing about the village is that there are several **tours** and **cruises** that begin there.

Many different companies offer **whale-watching cruises** from the end of December until April. They last from a couple of hours to a half-day and cost between $12 and $25 per person. There are so many trips to choose from that you don't have to make a reservation in advance. But if you want to find out about all the different options, check the newspaper for ads or ask at your hotel. One company that has very comfort-

The Port of Los Angeles has one of the world's largest artificial harbors and handles more cargo than any other port on the Pacific Coast.

Almost everything that is imported into the United States from Japan comes through the Port of Los Angeles.

able cruises is Los Angeles Harbor Cruise Company (213-831-0996). They, and lots of other companies, also offer **harbor tours** by boat. It's fun to see the ships in the harbor from another ship, and the guides are full of all kinds of information about the biggest, busiest port on the West Coast. Remember, if you are going on a cruise bring a warm jacket. Even if it is warm on land, it can be chilly on the water, especially out where the whales are.

Other tours you can take from the Ports of Call area include deep-sea fishing trips and cruises to Catalina Island (more about Catalina in chap. 13). You can even take a helicopter ride over Los Angeles.

You can get an excellent view of the harbor and the docks on your way to Long Beach. Take Harbor Boulevard from Ports of Call and follow the signs to the Vincent Thomas Bridge. This will take you over the water and give you a great view of everything. You'll probably even see the Love Boat down there somewhere among the aircraft carriers, tankers, and cargo ships. You will pass through Terminal Island where you will see acres and acres of shiny new Japanese cars, waiting to be distributed to dealers all over the United States. Notice the hundreds of oil wells, pumping up and down like preying mantises, right in the middle of everything, and the huge, round oil storage tanks everywhere. You really get a feeling for how much is shipped in and out of the country and how much energy it takes to make it all happen.

In Long Beach, follow the signs to the **Queen Mary** and the **Spruce Goose**. The Queen Mary was the most elegant ship of her time. She has

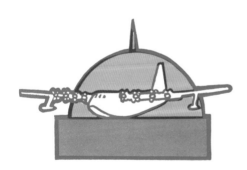

beautiful woodwork and appointments of the kind that just aren't made anymore. The ship is now a hotel and a very popular tourist attraction. A guided tour takes you from the cavernous engine room to the swimming pool and the first-class lounges and even the brig. During World War II, the Queen Mary was converted to a troop ship, carrying soldiers off to battle. There is a fascinating exhibit showing what life was like aboard the ship in those days.

Right next to the Queen, under a specially built geodesic dome, is the Spruce Goose, the largest airplane ever built. It was intended to carry troops during the war, too, but it only flew once (not too well). You can see a film of that flight and displays showing how the plane was built. You can climb a platform and see into the cockpit and the cargo area, which was designed to hold 750 soldiers. It's pretty impressive and probably the only time you will ever see an airplane with a wingspan longer than a football field.

Tickets to both the Spruce Goose and the Queen Mary are $16.50 for adults, $10.50 for kids. Those under 5 get in free. They are open 9:00 a.m. to 9:00 p.m. from July 4 to Labor Day and 10:00 a.m. to 6:00 p.m. the rest of the year. The phone number for more information is 213-435-3511.

In Long Beach, you might notice some pretty little islands not too far offshore. They are really oil wells decorated to look like islands.

6. Downtown

During the week, downtown Los Angeles is a busy, bustling place where tens of thousands of people (and their cars) go to work. The best time to visit is on a weekend when it's not very crowded, parking is easy, and you can really see what's there. And what's there is some of the most interesting and unusual architecture anywhere. Made of mirrors and marble and space age materials, some of the buildings give you an idea of what the future might look like.

Los Angeles is the only city in the United States that has a scent garden for the blind. You can smell it at 2830 W. 6th Street.

You can go inside the **Westin Bonaventure Hotel**, said to be the most futuristic hotel in the world. With its five mirrored towers and outside glass elevators, it looks like it might be a space station on some distant planet. The enormous lobby has a huge pool with beautiful fountains surrounded by hanging gardens and trees. Everything glitters and gleams. You can ride the elevators to the top, getting a fantastic view of the city below, visit the shops and restaurants, or just sit in the lobby and be amazed at the size of it all. The Bonaventure is at 404 S. Figueroa Street (213-524-1999).

In keeping with its adventurous spirit, Los Angeles has a long tradition of unusual, beautiful, or just plain crazy architecture, so as you

*Westin Bonaventure
Hotel*

*They call it "the stack,"
where the most traffic in
the world is said to pass
by everyday, 318 cars
every minute. It is east of
downtown where the
Santa Ana, Pomona, and
Garden State freeways
meet.*

travel around the city, get in the habit of looking at the buildings. Downtown, in addition to many fabulous new buildings, there are lots of old ones that are just great.

The **Coca-Cola Building** at 1334 S. Central looks like an ocean liner, even down to porthole windows and ship's doors, and is pretty amazing. So is the **Oviatt Building**, an art deco masterpiece with beautiful Lalique glass and lacy iron grillwork. There are lots of others, too.

You will want to visit the **Grand Central Market**—not for the building but for what is inside: more fruit and vegetables and meat and fish and exotic spices than you have ever imagined could be together in one place. Every day over 30,000 people come from all over L.A. to shop. The market is at Broadway and Hill streets and is open to the public 9 a.m.-6 p.m. Monday-Saturday (213-624-2378).

And if you think that was impressive, check out the **Los Angeles Flower Market** a few blocks away. This is a wholesale market where all the florists buy, but you can visit. The vendors are friendly, and where else can you see hundreds of thousands of tulips surrounded by what must be a million daisies? Not to mention the most exotic, amazing-looking flowers from the far corners of the earth. You can see all this at 9th and Hill Street. It's open Monday through Saturday, but you have to go early in the morning. By 10 a.m., the market is closed.

One place downtown that was made especially for kids is the **Los Angeles Children's Museum**. You can have a great time singing in the recording studio or performing for the camera in the television studio. There are art projects to work on and things to climb on and over and through. You can cast a crazy shadow in the Shadow Box room or build a wild sculpture in Sticky City and the Leggo Room. Everything here is designed for fun. The Children's Museum is at 310 Main Street (213-687-8800). It's open every weekend 10 a.m.-5 p.m., summer weekdays 11:30 a.m.-5 p.m., and on Wednesday and Thursday during the school year. Admission is $3 for everyone.

After you've seen the downtown of today, it's fun to go back in time and see what Los Angeles was like in the beginning after the first settlers came in 1781. Plan to spend some time at **El Pueblo de Los Angeles** just a few blocks from the

*Check out **City Hall**, a beauty in the Italian Classic style at Temple and Main streets. If you happen to be there during the week, go up to the observation deck on the 27th floor for an excellent view of downtown and beyond.*

Children's Museum in the area around Alameda, Sunset, and Main streets. Phone 213-628-1274.

El Pueblo is the site of the city's original settlement, where 44 men, women, and children, mostly blacks and Mexican Indians, established a small farming village right next to the native Indians who had been living in the area for centuries.

You can walk around on your own, but it is more interesting to take a walking tour with a guide who can tell you all about the history and the people. The tour begins at the Docent Center at 130 Paseo de la Plaza right next to the **Old Firehouse**. It takes about an hour and begins on the hour from 10 a.m.-1 p.m. Tuesday through Saturday. Among the buildings that give you an idea of the way people lived 150 or more years ago is the **Avila Adobe**, the oldest house in Los Angeles, built by the mayor of the town in 1818. Step outside and you are on **Olvera Street**, a Mexican market where you can shop for crafts and souvenirs, eat a taco or a burrito, and listen to mariachi music. The original **Plaza** with its wrought-iron bandstand and 100-year-old magnolia trees is at the end of the street. Be sure to read the plaque across from the kiosk. It tells about each of the first settlers, even the kids.

Not far from there, you can experience a completely different culture in **Little Tokyo**, the largest Japanese community outside of Japan, centered in the area around First Street from Main to Alameda. Head for the **Japanese Village Plaza Mall** for very Japanese architecture and lots of yummy Japanese food. The Mitsuru Children's Shop is full of toys and kites.

You can visit a garden in the sky at the **New**

Otani Hotel, First and Los Angeles streets. Take the elevator to the 5th floor and you are in a serene and beautiful Japanese world complete with trees and ponds and waterfalls. And you can see all of Los Angeles below you.

Nearby, at 704 Traction Avenue, is the **Museum of Neon Art** (213-617-1580), a wonderful little place full of signs and other things made with neon light, old and new. The display changes constantly. It doesn't take long to see, and if you are in the neighborhood, it's worth a visit. If you're lucky, you might get a glimpse of the dancing cow skeletons.

*Hungry for Chinese food? Then head for **Chinatown**, around the 900 block of N. Broadway, where you will find all you can eat and even a fortune cookie-making machine.*

7. Santa Monica

anta Monica is a nice little beachside city where a lot of kids live, and it's a good place for kids to visit. Most of the action is centered within a mile or so of the **Santa Monica Pier**.

Nearby, on the **Third Street Promenade** (3rd Street between Wilshire Boulevard and Broadway), huge topiary dinosaurs—made of trees—watch over the activity. You can see 14 different movies on the promenade, and there are many unusual shops and restaurants and special activities for families and kids scheduled from time to time. It's open every day and evening, too.

The Santa Monica Playhouse has special plays for kids, and their parents, every Saturday and Sunday at 1:00 p.m. and at 3:00 p.m. The plays change every few months and are very popular. You should try to make a reservation two weeks in advance. Tickets are $6 for everyone.

In the summer, the theater holds workshops where you can take acting classes or learn about makeup, costumes, sets, and music. The Playhouse is at 1211 4th Street (213-394-9779).

Angels Attic is in the oldest house in Santa Monica, a storybook Victorian built in 1875. Inside is a wonderful collection of dollhouses from all over the world. Many are very old, and all are fascinating in their intricate detail. There are dolls and stuffed animals, tiny and huge, and many other toys. You can have fancy tea or lemonade on the front porch and maybe feel that you have been sent back in time 100 years. Angels Attic is 5 blocks east of the Pier at 516 Colorado Avenue and is open Thursday-Sunday, 12:30 p.m. to 4:30 p.m. Admission is $3 for adults, $1 for kids (213-394-8331).

The Camera Obscura is a sort of periscope that lets you see the pier, the beach, and the street outside from a completely enclosed tower. It's all about mirrors and reflection. It's hard to explain, but it's worth seeing. It is located above the Senior Recreation Center in Palisades Park, 1450 Ocean Avenue, 3 blocks north of the Pier.

Palisades Park is a mile-long park that runs along the cliffs behind Santa Monica beach. You get a great view of the beach and the ocean. Sometimes you can see all the way to Catalina Island. It's a nice place to sit on a bench or under

*Did you ever think of going **ice skating** when the temperature is 80 degrees? You can try it at the **Culver Ice Rink,** 4545 Sepulveda Boulevard (213-398-5710), not far from Santa Monica in Culver City. It's open every day and most evenings and you can rent skates since you probably didn't bring them. It costs $3.75 to get in and $1.25 to rent skates. Call before you go, because they are sometimes closed for L.A. Kings hockey practice.*

Angels Attic

a tree and watch the world go by. If you listen, you will notice that people are speaking in lots of different foreign languages, a reminder of how many immigrants make their homes in Los Angeles.

If you like books, you will enjoy **Children's Book and Music Center**, which has a large selection of books on all subjects for children of all ages. There are also records, which you can listen to before you buy, and a good supply of musical instruments especially for kids. You will find books on tape and kid's videos and a very friendly and helpful staff. It's all at 2500 Santa Monica Boulevard, 213-829-0215, open Monday-Saturday 9 a.m.-5:30 p.m.

8. West Hollywood

West Hollywood, tucked between Hollywood and Beverly Hills, has some places that are fun to explore, and since it is near the Tar Pits (chap. 9), plan to go on the day you check out the sticky stuff.

The Farmers Market began with a small group of farmers who brought their harvest to a vacant lot at 3rd and Fairfax and sold it to the local residents. Today it is one of L.A.'s liveliest, friendliest places. It is a collection of little shops (160 of them) where you can buy anything from a live parrot to a pearl necklace to a teddy bear. And food. Farmers still bring fruits and vegetables, you can watch candy being made, or choose from over 100 different kinds of bread. There are restaurants that serve food from around the world. Everyone seems to be happy and relaxed

and having fun. It is a very popular tourist spot and can be crowded, but it's worth a visit. It's still at 3rd and Fairfax and is open Monday-Saturday 9 a.m.-6:30 p.m. (until 8 p.m. in the summer) and Sunday 10 a.m.-5 p.m. (213-933-9211).

Just up Fairfax, between Beverly and Melrose, is a very special area, the center of the Jewish community in Los Angeles. It is full of delicatessens, kosher grocery stores, bakeries, and produce stands. Many signs are in Hebrew, and shops sell religious articles and Jewish gifts. It is not unusual to see Orthodox men wearing long black coats and tall black hats walking to one of the neighborhood synagogues.

If you turn right on **Melrose Avenue** and go just a few blocks, you are in a completely different world and on L.A.'s trendiest street. This is where the newest and the hottest and often the wildest is found. It's fun to walk around for a bit and watch the people, some of them dressed in fairly outrageous garb. There are many fashionable stores and shops to browse in and plenty to eat, from a full meal to an Italian ice cream cone.

If you travel down Melrose in the other direction (west), you will encounter one of L.A.'s favorite new buildings, the **Blue Whale**, an enormous structure made entirely of shiny, bright blue tiles. Next to it is a huge, shiny green building that hasn't been around long enough to acquire a nickname. Under construction is the third member of the triumvirate, which is going to be ruby red. They are all part of the **Pacific Design Center**, a showcase of interest to interior designers and architects, on the corner of Melrose and San Vicente.

If you go south on San Vicente to the corner of Beverly Boulevard, you can eat a hot dog at a hot dog at **The Tail O' the Pup.** The building is a hot dog on a bun, and it is a classic because it is one of the only ones of its kind left. L.A. used to have lots of buildings in the shape of what they sold: doughnut shops shaped like doughnuts, shoe repair places that looked like a shoe, ice cream stands like ice cream cones, and the famous Brown Derby restaurant, shaped like a hat. Most have been torn down to make way for office buildings or mini-malls, but the hot dog was saved. So have a hot dog and know that you are eating a bit of Los Angeles history.

Your visit to West Hollywood would not be complete without a trip down the famous **Sunset Strip**, a two-mile section of Sunset Boulevard

between Fairfax and Doheny. Once the center of glamorous L.A. nightlife, today it houses the offices of movie producers, agents, and publicity people. The fun is in seeing the enormous billboards that tower over the street promoting the latest movie and the hottest records. Some are three-dimensional and seem to reach out and grab you. You really feel that you are in Movieland. Don't be surprised when you encounter an oceanliner sailing across Sunset Boulevard. It's just another example of L.A.'s architectural craziness called the **Crossroads of the World**.

9. Museums

Sometimes kids are not too excited by the idea of going to museums. But in Los Angeles, there are a few museums that are so special, interesting, or fun that you just have to check them out.

Imagine it's 40,000 thousand years ago and you are a giant ground sloth wandering through the forest that was then Los Angeles. You are hot and thirsty and you come across a shining pool. You step in and take a drink and Yuk!, it's not water, it's sticky, gooky tar. You try to back out but you're stuck and sinking. You panic, you sink deeper and deeper and very shortly disappear. Soon the surface is shiny and smooth again, waiting for the next victim. This little drama was repeated literally millions of times as animals large and small were lured to their death in the **La Brea Tar Pits**.

Today scientists have extracted the bones and reconstructed many of these exotic animals. Dyed a deep, shiny brown by the tar, the skeletons look like bronze sculptures. You can see them at the **George Page Museum of La Brea Discoveries**. The museum is at 5801 Wilshire Boulevard (213-936-2230). It's open Tuesday-Sunday 10 a.m.-5 p.m. and costs $1.50; half-price for people under 18.

You can see the tar pits themselves, watch the excavations still going on, and observe technicians cleaning and assembling the bones in the laboratory. There is a movie about the excavations and you can actually fool around with the gluey stuff at the "Asphalt Is Sticky" exhibit. There is no place in the world like this so don't miss it.

Have you ever wondered what it would have been like to be a pioneer kid crossing the country with your folks in a covered wagon? And what life was like when you got to a brand new town in the Wild West? What made men want to be cowboys, anyway? You can find out about all this and more at the **Gene Autry Western Heritage Museum**. This is L.A.'s newest museum. It's full of everything you ever wanted to know about the Old West and really makes it all come alive. The exhibits are colorful and bright and easy to understand. There are several movies and videos and special effects and great collections of everything from clothing (notice how much smaller people were then) to guns to furniture to kids' toys.

There is a lot about horses including a couple of the fanciest silver saddles you have ever seen. And since Gene Autry was a famous movie cowboy in the 1940s and 50s, it's not surprising that movie and TV westerns have a big place here. The stars and their costumes, horses, and sidekicks are all displayed. This museum is definitely wonderful, even if you didn't think you were interested in cowboys. The museum is in Griffith Park, directly in front of the entrance to the zoo. It is open Tuesday-Sunday 10 a.m.-5 p.m. Tickets cost $4.75 for adults, $2.00 for kids under 12 (213-667-2000).

You can find out about the other side of the cowboys and Indians story at the **Southwest Museum,** where Indians are the theme. When the Spanish came to what is now Los Angeles in 1781, there were Native Americans all over the area, living a peaceful and fairly comfortable life. They had plenty to eat since they were surrounded by fish and wildlife, and they made beautiful baskets that they filled with wild plants, nuts, and berries. They decorated their clothing with beads made from shells, created beautiful carvings and other artwork, and traded with their neighbors, even traveling back and forth to Catalina Island in canoes. Religion was a very important part of their lives, for they believed that God and Spirit was in nature all around them, which they celebrated in ceremony and ritual as part of daily living.

The Spanish arrived with their own religion, Christianity, to which they felt it was their duty to convert the "heathen" Indians. They built missions wherever they went and forced the natives to adopt the new God. Those who refused to go

Notice how the Indians around Los Angeles used tar from the tar pits in their daily lives, for everything from sealing containers to waterproofing canoes. And be sure to take the creaky elevator downstairs to the mysterious tunnel.

along were enslaved: shackled, whipped, even branded like cattle. The Spanish brought new diseases, too, like measles and smallpox, which wiped out huge numbers of Indians. It wasn't too long before Indian culture in California was destroyed and now we can only see it in museums.

The Southwest Museum is full of Indian things and stories and gives us a good idea of what life was like for them, not just in California but all over the Southwest. It is small, and you can see it all in an hour. It is well worth the trip. Check out the beaded papooses, baby carriers very similar to the kind we use today.   The Southwest Museum is at 234 Museum Drive in Highland Park, north of downtown. It's open Tuesday-Sunday 11 a.m.-5 p.m. and costs $3 for adults, $1 for kids. Don't forget about the tunnel.

The Griffith Observatory and Planetarium in

Griffith Park sits high on a hill overlooking Los Angeles. On a clear day, you get a spectacular view all the way to the ocean. On a smoggy day, you can get a good idea of exactly how bad L.A.'s famous smog really is. Inside you can see a pendulum demonstrate the rotation of the earth, watch speeding steel balls show you how gravity works, and see several exhibits about the solar system. In the Planetarium a huge projector creates the night sky as it looks from anywhere on earth. Planetarium shows change regularly and are exciting as well as interesting. At night you can look at the real stars through the large telescope or see the **Laserium** show, a music and light show created with fantastic multicolored laser beams. The Observatory is free and open afternoons and evenings year-round. There is charge for the Planetarium and Laserium shows; their times vary, so call for a schedule. Get there through the Vermont Ave. entrance to the park and call 213-664-1191 for show times and prices.

You will see a completely different kind of

show at the **IMAX Theater** where a movie screen 5 stories high and 70 feet wide makes you feel as if you are really in the picture. You're riding the rapids of the Colorado River, flying an F-15 jet, or piloting the space shuttle high above the earth. There are several different movies shown at different times during the day, so call ahead (213-774-7400) for times. Tickets cost $4.75 for adults and $3 for kids.

The IMAX is on the grounds of the **California Museum of Science and Industry**, next to the Coliseum. The museum has a number of "interactive" exhibits, which means you can actually do things instead of just look. Don't miss the demonstration of how an earthquake really feels and how it is caused. You can design a bike on a computer or use it to create a work of art. In the **Hall of Health** you get your own personal "credit card" that you put into machines that test your blood pressure and stress level, your balance, and your eating habits. The **Aerospace Museum** has the real Gemini ll space capsule, a copy of the space shuttle, a communications satellite, and even a bicycle-powered flying machine.

The **Museum of Afro-American History and Culture** has displays and information about black American contributions in all areas of American life. You will find all this and more, for free, at the museum complex located at Exposition Boulevard and Figueroa Street. Open daily 10 a.m.-5 p.m. (213-774-7400).

The **Getty Museum** was built by J. Paul Getty, one of the richest men in the world, to hold his own collection of art. The building itself is interesting since it is copy of a country house owned by a wealthy family in ancient Rome. The real

house was buried when Mt. Vesuvius erupted almost two thousand years ago.

The first floor is filled with antiquities, which means things that were made a very long time ago, in this case as many as 4,000 years. Some are so valuable that they have their own special earthquake protection systems that cost over $1 million.

The upstairs is full of beautiful things made in the seventeenth and eighteenth centuries, especially furniture and other household stuff.

The Getty is high up on a cliff at 17985 Pacific Coast Highway. It is open Tuesday-Sunday from 10 a.m.-5 p.m. It's free, but you have to make a reservation in advance to park your car or arrange to park down below and take a shuttle bus up. Call 213-459-2003.

Be sure you visit the mummy masks. These are full-color paintings of people who were buried inside mummy cases. You might be surprised to find one that looks a lot like your grandmother, your uncle, or even yourself.

You can explore the area around the pool where the walls are painted to fool your eye into thinking that there are grapevines and trees and other plants there. That style of painting is called **trompe l'oeil** *(pronounced like trump loo-eel).*

10. Parks, Gardens, and Other Outdoor Fun

The main park in Los Angeles is **Griffith Park,** and it is huge. In fact, it covers an entire mountain, front and back, and it's right in the middle of Los Angeles. There are four different entrances to the park, each leading to a different area. Inside are miles of hiking trails and many wonderful picnic spots and places to explore, including a bird sanctuary and a mini-forest of ferns. The **Zoo,** the **Planetarium,** and the **Gene Autry Museum** (see chap. 9 for more about the last two) are all within the park. You can play tennis (call 213-662-7772 for information), and there are several places to rent and ride horses. Try Griffith Park Livery Stables (818-840-8401) or Circle K Stables (818-843-9890), both in Burbank, or Sunset Ranch (213-464-9612) on the Hollywood side.

Travel Town calls itself a transportation museum, but it seems more like a place to climb and explore. It's full of old railroad cars and steam engines that you can get in and climb all over. On Sunday, from noon to 4 p.m., members of the Los Angeles Live Steamers Club run their own miniature steam engines on a track next to Travel Town. You can ride them for free. Travel Town is free, too, and open every day from 10

Kidspace is near Huntington Gardens. Here you can put on the outfit of an astronaut, a jockey, a football player, whatever you would like to be. The Dr. Feelbetter exhibit shows you all about your body in a very fun way. You can talk with Herman the resident robot or work in a kid-size TV station. Kidspace is at 390 S. El Molino Avenue in Pasadena and is open Wednesday 2 p.m.-5 p.m. and Saturday and Sunday noon to 5 p.m. There are special hours during school vacations. It costs $2.50. Call ahead to get directions and to find out what special things are going on (818-449-9144).

a.m. until 4 p.m. weekdays and until 5 p.m. on weekends. It is at the beginning of Zoo Drive (213-662-5874).

A little farther along Zoo Drive, you will come to, surprise, the **Los Angeles County Zoo**, which has more than 2,000 animals from all over the world. They all live in their own habitats that are meant to be as similar as possible to the places they would live in the wild. Hardly any, except the birds and the reptiles, are actually in cages. The animals are grouped according to continent, so you can visit Africa or South America or Australia. The zoo is very concerned with saving endangered species, and there is information about which animals are in danger of becoming extinct and why. The **Children's Zoo** lets you get close to animals, and there is a nursery where all kinds of baby animals are fed from bottles. There are plenty of food stands, so you won't go hungry even if you stay a long time. The zoo is open every day from 10 a.m.-5 p.m. and until 6 p.m. in the summer. The fee is $4.50 for adults, $1.50 for kids (213-666-4090). (The Gene Autry Museum

is right across the street; you can see both in a day.)

You can see things that you can't see anywhere else at the Cactus Garden at **Huntington Gardens**, just 12 miles from downtown. You can walk among cactus trees that are 50 feet tall and barrel cacti a yard wide. You will probably notice that each one seems to have its own personality, and they are clever at protecting themselves with those killer thorns. And such blossoms—they look like they were dreamed up by Walt Disney.

Actually, the rest of Huntington Gardens is pretty special, too. There are acres of thick, green lawns for running and rolling, huge trees to sit under and look up into, thousands of rose bushes, and what seems like every kind of flower and plant on earth. There is a Japanese garden and a real Japanese house. There is also a restaurant, an enormous mansion, and a library full of special books, including the first book ever printed with movable type, the Gutenberg Bible. All this used to belong to one man, Henry Huntington, who made a fortune owning trains in Los Angeles and loved to plant plants. It's all free and open Tuesday-Sunday from 1 p.m.-4:30 p.m. If you want to go on Sunday, you must make a reservation in advance. It's at 1151 Oxford Road in San Moreno; 818-405-2100.

If you visit Los Angeles between May and September and crave a wet and crazy adventure, head for **Raging Waters** about 40 minutes south of L.A. Here you will find all kinds of water activities—from tame to wild—with more than 100 lifeguards watching over it all. You can bring a picnic or buy food at several snack bars. Bring your own towels and plenty of sunscreen; they

have lockers and dressing rooms. Beginning in early May, Raging Waters is open 10 a.m.-6 p.m. on weekends. From early June into September, it is open 7 days a week, 9 a.m.-10 p.m. The number of people allowed in at any one time is limited for safety reasons. So get there early. Tickets are $14.50; people under 48 inches tall, $8.50. It costs $2 to park. Call 714-592-8181.

There are three other big theme parks near Los Angeles. They are all about an hour drive out of town and all feature enough attractions, rides, and adventures to easily take up a whole day. (You can call for directions.)

Of course, everyone has heard of **Disneyland**. Hours vary with the seasons so call ahead. Admission to everything is $16.50 for adults, $10.50 for children under 12. Children under 3, free. Parking is $2. Telephone 714-999-4000.

Knott's Berry Farm is also in Anaheim and also has hours that change with the time of year. In addition to 164 rides, shows, and attractions, you can take a ride on a man-made white water river. It's $12.95 for adults and $9.95 for kids. Children under 3 get in free, and there is no charge for parking. Telephone 714-826-1776.

Going in the other direction from L.A., also on I-5, is **Magic Mountain**. Here you find more action rides and performances than theme shows, and some are pretty scary. Magic Mountain is heaven for roller coaster lovers. If that's not enough, there are also high diving shows, dolphin shows, and Bugs Bunny park for the younger ones. Hours vary. Adults pay $13.95; people under 4 feet tall get in for half price. Telephone 818-367-5965.

11. Sports

L os Angeles is pure pleasure for sports fans. Every professional sport is played here so no matter when you visit you can go to a game of something.

From April through October, you can see a **Dodger** baseball game at **Dodger Stadium** where every one of the 56,000 seats is a good one because there are no posts to block your view. Tickets cost from $8-$5 for adults and $3-$4 for kids. It's $3 to park your car. The stadium is just north of downtown at 1000 Elysian Park Avenue. For information call 213-224-1500; for tickets call 213-224-1400.

You can see Magic Johnson rack up the points when the **Los Angeles Lakers** are at home at **The Forum** from November through April. Tickets go from $8.50-$60. The forum is at Manchester and Prairie in Inglewood. The box office number is 213-419-3182. LA's other NBA team, the **Clippers**, play at the **L.A. Sports Arena** at 3939 S. Figueroa, 213-748-6131. Tickets cost $6-$18.

The Forum is also the home of the **Los Angeles Kings** hockey team. They play from October through April and tickets range from $7-$18. You can see an indoor soccer game at the

The Los Angeles Dodgers were the first California baseball team ever to win a World Series. They did it in 1960.

The Olympic victory stand, where athletes receive their medals, was invented at the 1932 Olympics held at the Coliseum.

The Coliseum was the site of the 1984 Olympics, too.

The first Superbowl ever was held at the Coliseum in January 1967.

Forum, too, when the **Los Angeles Lazers** play from November through April. Tickets are $16. The Forum also hosts world-class **tennis,** championship **boxing, rodeos, ice skating, the Harlem Globetrotters**, and a wide range of other sports and entertainment events. Call 213-673-1300 to find out what's happening when you are in town.

For football fans, the **Los Angeles Raiders** play at the **L.A. Memorial Coliseum** from September through December. The coliseum is next to the Sports Arena at 3911 S. Figueroa (213-322-5901).

If you love horses, you might want to check out the morning workouts at **Santa Anita Racetrack**. During racing season from December through April, you can watch the thoroughbreds go through their paces in the mornings from

7:30 to 9:30 on race days, which are Wednesday through Sunday. As the horses drill, the announcer gives their names and times. On Saturday and Sunday mornings, you can even take a tour through the stables with a friendly guide who tells you all about the routine and care of the several hundred horses who live there. The workouts and tour are free, and you can have breakfast at the track restaurant. The track is in Arcadia at 285 W. Huntington Drive. Telephone 818-574-7223.

If you would like to see a **polo match**, you can catch the **Los Angeles Stars** professional team at the **Los Angeles Equestrian Center** in Burbank on most Saturdays from March to June and September to December. General admission costs $7.50 and box seats are $20. The center also has horse shows and other horsey activities. It is on Riverside Drive at Main Street in Burbank. Call them for a schedule at 818-840-9063.

More informal polo matches happen on most weekends when the weather is good at **Will Rogers State Park** at 14253 Sunset Boulevard. Polo is free, but you have to pay $3 to park.

During World War II, Santa Anita Racetrack was used as a camp for Japanese prisoners of war.

12. Music, Theater, and the Hollywood Bowl

Would you like to hear a big philharmonic orchestra or maybe a concert by your favorite rock band? How about a play, a Broadway musical, or a ballet? It's all available in Los Angeles, and the best place to find out what is going on in town is the newspaper, particularly the Calendar section of the *Los Angeles Times*. On Sunday, the Calendar is a huge magazine full of everything going on that week, including a section on special activities just for kids.

If you visit L.A. in the summer, be sure to go to the **Hollywood Bowl**. It is an enormous outdoor amphitheater where most people bring, or buy, a picnic to eat under the trees before the performance. On the 4th of July and at other times, there are fireworks during the performance. The Los Angeles Philharmonic Orchestra performs there, as do many other musical groups, from July to September. Ticket prices vary, and you can almost always sit up at the top for $1. This is one of the few places in L.A. that is easy to get to by bus. Special buses go from all over town directly to the Bowl and back. The bus number is 213-860-2000. The Bowl number is 213-850-2000, and the address is 2301 N. Highland in the Hollywood Hills.

Hollywood Bowl

For a cozier outdoor concert, try the **Greek Theater**, on Vermont Avenue in Griffith Park. Designed to resemble an amphitheater in ancient Greece, it's a favorite spot for summer pop and rock concerts. It is open from May to October and ticket prices vary. Call the box office for information, weekdays 10 a.m.-6 p.m.

The winter home of the Philharmonic is the **Dorothy Chandler Pavilion**, which, combined with the **Mark Taper Forum** and the **Ahmanson Theater**, make up the **Music Center**, the center for performing arts in L.A. Concerts, theater, musicals, dance, opera, and more all happen at the Music Center. It is a huge and beautiful complex with a wonderful pulsating fountain that rhythmically shoots 100 streams of water into the air. Even if you don't go to a performance at the Center, you can see it on a free tour. Call 213-972-7483 for tour information and reservations. For information about performances at the Music Center, call 213-972-7211. The Music Center is at 135 Grand Avenue, downtown.

One very special show for kids happens at the **Bob Baker Marionette Theater**, where you sit on the floor and watch the marionettes come to life before your eyes. After the show, you can visit backstage and learn how the marionettes are made and operated. Shows are Saturdays and Sundays at 2:30 p.m. Tickets are $6 for adults and $5 for kids. You have to make a reservation by calling 213-250-9995. The theater is at 1345 W. 1st Street, downtown.

13. Excursions out of Town

Although there is plenty to keep you busy in Los Angeles, there are also some adventures to be had by taking a short trip out of town.

How about a train ride? You can take a day trip to **Santa Barbara** or **San Juan Capistrano** on a speedy **Amtrak** train.

The trip up the coast to Santa Barbara takes about two hours, just enough time to explore the train, chat with the conductor, and watch the world outside race past your window.

The Santa Barbara train station is on State Street, the main shopping area, full of shops and restaurants and some historic buildings. At the foot of State Street, you will find the beach and the pier, here called **Stearn's Wharf**. If you don't feel like walking, you can rent a pedi-cab or take the Santa Barbara Trolley.

Or you could take the train south to visit the **Mission San Juan Capistrano,** one of the original missions, built by the Spanish in 1797. The beautiful chapel is the oldest building in California, and you can explore the surrounding area, which has archaeological sites, gardens, and an Indian cemetery, a memorial to the Indian slaves who built the mission. The museum has

Every year, on March 19, the swallows return to the San Juan Capistrano Mission to spend the summer. They have been coming for as long as anyone can remember and tourists and bird watchers flock to welcome them. On October 23, they leave and fly to South America for the winter. How they know the date is one of nature's mysteries.

Mission San Juan Capistrano

Catalina Island was originally part of Baja California. It broke off and drifted north and out to sea several million years ago.

Over the years, Catalina has been a favorite hideout for pirates and smugglers and bootleggers who knew all the secret coves and hiding places.

exhibits of Indian and Spanish life. The mission is right across from the train station, and there is a restaurant nearby if you want a bite to eat before heading back to L.A.

The trains leave from Union Station downtown, right across from El Pueblo de Los Angeles. The Santa Barbara train leaves at 9:55 a.m. and heads back to L.A. at 4:50 p.m. Tickets are $26 round-trip, half-price for people under 12. There are 8 departures for San Juan Capistrano every day and as many coming back. It costs $20 round-trip, half-price for kids. Amtrak reservations and information number is 213-624-0171.

Have you always wanted to take a cruise? You can get a feel for it on a trip 22 miles out in the Pacific to **Catalina Island**. Keep your eyes out for flying fish along the way. You will land at Avalon, the only town on the island, where you can walk to wherever you are going. Head for the Pleasure Pier and the Chamber of Commerce for a complete rundown of all there is to see and do. You can actually see what goes on underwater on the **Glass Bottom Boat Cruise.** Or get a glimpse of sea lions and other wildlife on the 45-minute **Coastal Cruise**. You can rent bikes and explore the town or just hang out at the beach and play in the calm blue water. Inland, you can see a herd of small buffalo, relatives of the ones brought to the island by a movie company 60 years ago.

Catalina is a good spot for a day trip or you can stay longer at one of the island's many hotels.

Boats depart from San Pedro and Long Beach and cost $20-$25 for adults, $10-$15 for people under 12. Try Catalina Express (213-519-1212) or

Catalina Cruises (213-775-6111). You can also helicopter to Catalina for $80 per person with Helitrans Helicopter Service (213-548-1314).

A trip to the mountains is a nice change of pace, and you can drive to **Big Bear** and **Lake Arrowhead** in a couple of hours. The mountain views from the Rim of the World Highway are fantastic. In the winter this is a ski area, and in the summer it has boating, fishing, horseback riding, and plenty of woods to explore. You can take the **chair lift** on a 20-minute ride up to 8,600 feet, and the **Moonridge Animal Park** has some of the black bears for which the area was named. You can make it a day trip or stay longer at one of the many hotels and lodges. Call 714-866-5877 for lodging information. Get there by taking I-10 east to I-15E. Exit Sierra Way and follow Highway 18 up the mountains.

Catalina was home to the Gabrielenos Indians for more than 2,000 years. They worshiped the sun, lived on fish and native plants, and traveled back and forth to the mainland by canoe. They were finally killed, along with all of the sea otters, by Russian fur traders in the 1800s.

Calendar of Events

January

Tournament of Roses Parade and Rose Bowl game on New Year's Day in Pasadena.

Disney On Ice at the Sports Arena featuring Mickey and all his buddies.

February

Chinese New Year parade and fireworks in Chinatown, downtown L.A.

International Folk Dance Festival at the Music Center. Dances from around the world with magicians and jugglers,too.

March

Academy Awards Presentations at the Shrine Auditorium. Bleachers are set up outside for the public to watch the stars arrive.

Grunion run season begins.

Los Angeles Marathon.

Beverly Hills St. Patrick's Day parade. They roll out the green carpet and have a star-studded, funny parade.

April

Easter sunrise services at the Hollywood Bowl.

Traditional Mexican Blessing of the Animals on Olvera Street.

Kite Festival, Santa Monica beach.

May

Cinco de Mayo celebration on Olvera Street with dancing, music, and merrymaking.

UCLA Mardi Gras Fair with games, food, and entertainment.

Memorial Day Classic Horse Show at Griffith Park Equestrian Center. A 6-day event with riders competing for $15,000 in prize money.

June
Folk Art Festival at the L.A. County Natural History Museum with crafts, exhibits, dancing, music, and ethnic foods.

All-City Outdoor Arts Festival in Barnsdall Park, featuring puppet shows and other performances.

July
Fireworks at various locations all over Los Angeles.

International Surf Festival at Redondo, Manhattan, and Hermosa beaches.

Fiddle and banjo contest with clog dancing, square dancing, and Scottish dancing at UCLA athletic field.

Body Building Championships at Muscle Beach in Venice.

August
Malibu World Cup Surfing Championships at Zuma Beach.

Women's Pro Volleyball competition at Will Rogers State Beach in Santa Monica.

Nisei Week in Little Tokyo honors Japanese-American culture with parades, music, dancing, martial arts demonstrations, even tea ceremonies.

September
Los Angeles County Fair, the biggest county fair in the United States.

Mexican Independence Day Fiesta around Olvera Street.

Los Angeles Street Scene, a two-day multicultural celebration held in downtown streets with food, music, dancing, crafts and exhibits.

October
International Beach Volleyball Classic starring two-man volleyball teams from around the world at Santa Monica beach.

Annual Santa Monica Pier Kite Festival.

November
Hollywood Christmas Parade with Santa and lots of movie and television stars.

Doo Dah Parade in Pasadena parodies the Rose Bowl Parade.

December
Marina del Rey Christmas Boat Parade.

Los Posadas traditional Mexican Christmas candlelight processions and piñata breaking.

For more detailed information, contact the Los Angeles Visitors and Convention Bureau, 515 S. Figueroa Street, Los Angeles 90071, 213-624-7300.

Kidding Around with John Muir Publications

We are making the world more accessible for young travelers. In your hand you have one of several John Muir Publications guides written and designed especially for kids. We will be *Kidding Around* other cities also. Send us your thoughts, corrections, and suggestions. We also publish other books about travel and other subjects. Let us know if you would like one of our catalogs.

John Muir Publications
P.O. Box 613
Santa Fe, New Mexico 87504
(505) 982-4078